Everyday Computing with Windows 8.1

Kevin Wilson

Apress®

Everyday Computing with Windows 8.1

ISBN-13 (pbk): 978-1-4842-0806-9

ISBN-13 (electronic): 978-1-4842-0805-2

Managing Director: Welmoed Spahr
Lead Editor: Steve Anglin
Editorial Board: Steve Anglin, Mark Beckner, Ewan Buckingham, Gary Cornell, Louise Corrigan, Jim DeWolf, Jonathan Gennick, Robert Hutchinson, Michelle Lowman, James Markham, Matthew Moodie, Jeff Olson, Jeffrey Pepper, Douglas Pundick, Ben Renow-Clarke, Dominic Shakeshaft, Gwenan Spearing, Matt Wade, Steve Weiss
Coordinating Editor: Christine Ricketts
Compositor: SPi Global
Indexer: SPi Global
Artist: SPi Global
Cover Designer: Anna Ishchenko

Distributed to the book trade worldwide by Springer Science+Business Media New York, 233 Spring Street, 6th Floor, New York, NY 10013. Phone 1-800-SPRINGER, fax (201) 348-4505, e-mail orders-ny@springer-sbm.com, or visit www.springeronline.com. Apress Media, LLC is a California LLC and the sole member (owner) is Springer Science + Business Media Finance Inc (SSBM Finance Inc). SSBM Finance Inc is a Delaware corporation.

For information on translations, please e-mail rights@apress.com, or visit www.apress.com.

Apress and friends of ED books may be purchased in bulk for academic, corporate, or promotional use. eBook versions and licenses are also available for most titles. For more information, reference our Special Bulk Sales–eBook Licensing web page at www.apress.com/bulk-sales.

Any source code or other supplementary material referenced by the author in this text is available to readers at www.apress.com. For detailed information about how to locate your book's source code, go to www.apress.com/source-code/.

Contents at a Glance

Contents

About the Author

Kevin Wilson, a practicing computer engineer and tutor, has been a computer buff for many years. After graduating with a master's degree in computer science, software engineering and multimedia systems, he has worked in the computer industry supporting and working with many different types of computer systems, worked in education running specialist lessons on film making and visual effects for young people.

He has also worked as an IT Tutor, has taught in colleges in South Africa and worked as a tutor for adult education in England.

Chapter 1

About Windows

Windows is the operating system that runs the software that runs IBM PC compatible computers, laptops and a slightly modified version that runs Windows Phones. Window 8.1 is used for most of the examples in this book. So, Windows is in essence the program that runs your computer. There are other operating systems, UNIX (Linux) also runs on PCs; Apple Mac computers have their own operating system which can also run Windows. Android is an operating system for phones, as is iOS for Apple's iPhones. But this book is about Windows based PCs, which account for the great majority of PCs.

Windows displays the applications (software) on your device. It also stores all of your files: documents, videos, pictures, music and so others. It enables you to locate and then click on them to open them. It also provides for many other aspects of running your computer including logging in (with or without a password), shutting down, and so on.

Windows 8 was a radical redesign of the Windows interface; it saw the introduction of a new Start screen that replaced the beloved Start menu in Windows 7 and prior versions of Windows. The figure below shows the Windows Desktop. The Desktop has been retained in Windows 8/8.1 but it is now found in the Start screen.

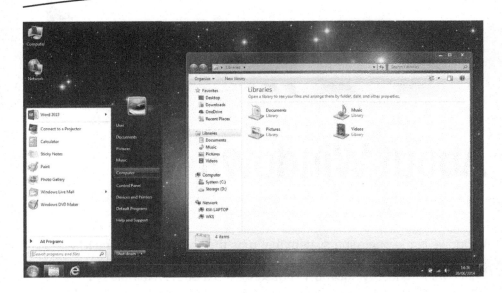

The first thing you will notice when you open Windows 8 is the Start screen. It displays your applications as colorful tiles. The idea is that you click on the tile to launch the application. To do so, simply move your mouse over the tile and click on Enter. If you have a touch screen, you can simply touch the tile to open it.

Note the Desktop is still available in Windows 8 as we saw before, but you have to click on the Desktop tile on the Start screen to access it (third down on the left on this computer). You can change the tiles around on the Start screen, so yours probably looks a little different.

Windows 8 was primarily designed for touch screens and mobile devices such as tablets and Microsoft's own touch screen Surface laptop/tablet hybrid style devices.

Also introduced in Windows 8.1 is the Charms bar; this allows you to access different settings such as preferences and the Control Panel. We will discuss these in the coming chapters.

These settings were previously accessible from the Start menu in Windows 7, so the Start menu takes a little getting used to if you are an old Windows user.

Microsoft also has the Windows Phone. The Windows Phone uses an altered version of Windows 8 to run on a phone. It has Windows 8's Start screen which allows you to open apps by tapping on the colored tiles. So Microsoft, as you can see, is moving toward seamless integration between their phone, and computers.

Now that we have a sense of the Windows operating system that runs the computer, the next chapter will focus on hardware and setting up your computer.

Chapter 2

Setting Up Your Device

This chapter will show you how to set up your computer. First you should set your machine up on a firm desk.

1. Insert the battery if it is not already connected.

2. Connect the power.

3. Plug the cord into the side of your laptop and press the power button.

I will be using my laptop for this example.

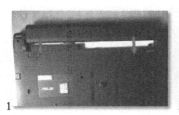

You will no doubt come across connectors called USB ports, they let you connect mice, printers, scanners, cameras and any other accessories you can think of to your computer quickly and easily.

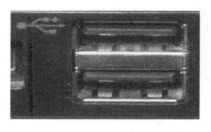

You usually have some USB ports on the back of your machine; these are good for connecting devices you can leave permanently plugged in.

You may also find some USB ports on the front of your machine. These are good for connecting removable media such as external hard disks and USB memory sticks. These allow you to save or download data out to or from the connected device.

Laptops will have USB ports on the sides of the machine.

Starting Windows 8 for the First Time

If your computer is not already set up, you will need to go through the setup process. You should follow the instructions provided but this will give you a quick look at the Windows 8 setup process.

Step 1 – Pick a language

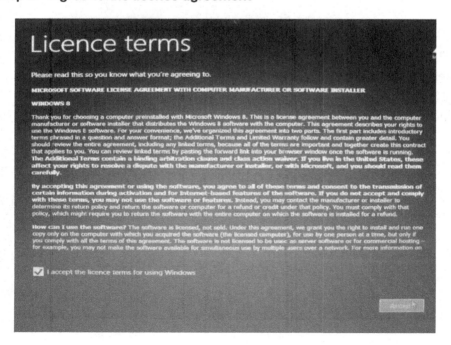

Step 2 – Agree to the licence agreement

Step 3 – Personalize your copy of Windows 8

Pick a color – I'm going to go with blue.

PC name – This is useful if you have more than one PC in the house. A good strategy is to name the PC according to either who is using it or what room it's in. I'm going to go with KW-Laptop, because I am using Windows 8 on my laptop. Other examples: ClairesLaptop, PC-Study, PC-livingroom, etc.

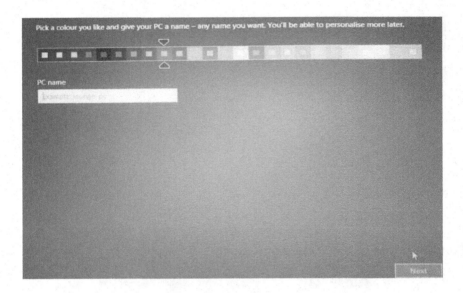

Personal

Step 4 – Set up your wireless internet

Windows 8 will automatically scan for nearby wireless routers. It is just a matter of finding the name of yours in the list. The name of your wireless internet is called the SSID and will be written on the back of your router.

Step 5 – Configure your settings

I would go with express settings. This allows Windows 8 to configure the settings for you.

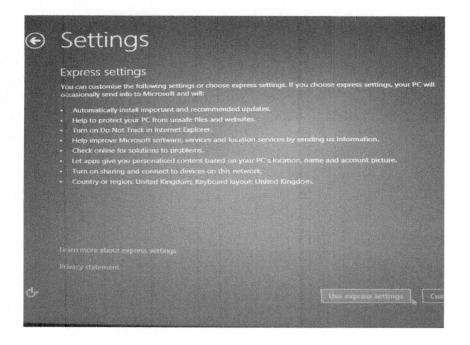

Step 6 – Create a Microsoft account

Click Microsoft account below and follow the instructions on the screen. A Microsoft account gives you access to email, Windows store, and a lot more than a local account. We will cover Microsoft accounts in Chapter 13.

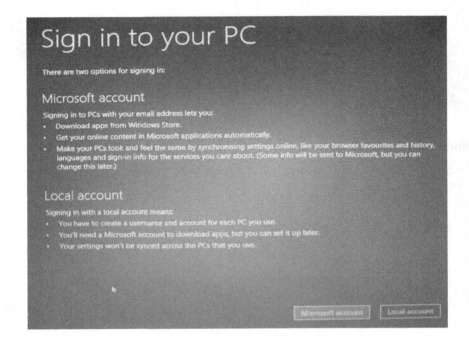

Chapter 3

Transferring your Old Files

The chances are, you will want to transfer files from your old computer, backups, or off of memory sticks. This chapter focuses on taking files off your old computer and then putting them on your new one. You can also use a cable to send files from one computer to another or you can use a network connection, but using an external drive or memory stick is simple and has the added benefit of giving you a copy of your data. The bottom line is that if there is a problem, then if you are just copying files, then it is harder to mess up.

Off your Old Computer

The process we will outline here is to use an external drive to collect the files from your old computer and then connect to the new computer to load them there. First, connect the external drive to your old computer. If you are using Windows 7, click on the **Start** button and type **Windows Easy Transfer** and then click on its search result when it appears. Windows Easy Transfer should now be open as shown below. In our example, we will use Windows 7 as the old operating system and Windows 8.1 as the new.

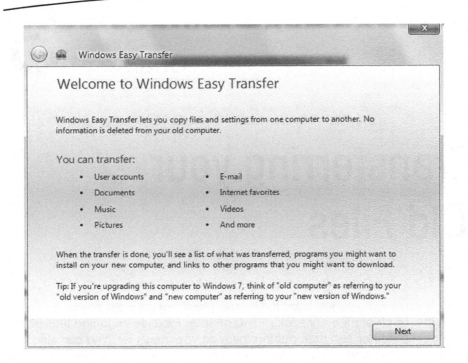

Note that Windows Easy Transfer makes it simple to copy your settings internet favorites, your passwords and your email. These are items that are a lot trickier to accomplish if you were to try to just copy your files from one computer to another. So you do not have to worry about where they are coming from.

Click on the **Next** button and you will be at a screen where you will select how you wish to transfer your data. Click on an **external hard disk or USB flash drive**.

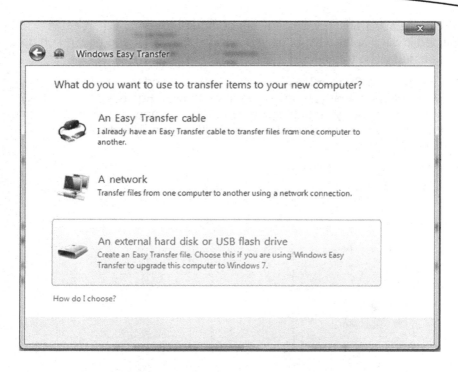

Click on **This is my old computer** button.

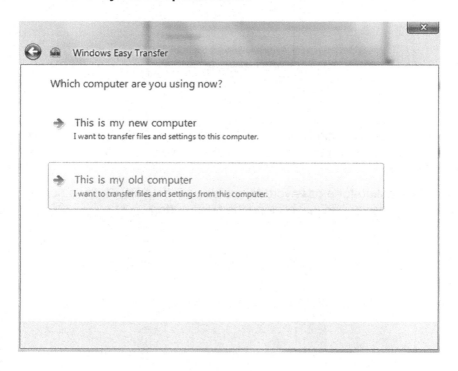

Windows Easy Transfer will scan your computer for data. When it has finished it will display a list of all users on the computer and how much data is expected to be transferred.

You can use the **Customize** link under each user and under Shared Items to leave out items that you do not want to transfer. For instance, you may not want to transfer your settings from your old computer to new. Choosing Customize will bring up a small screen similar to the following.

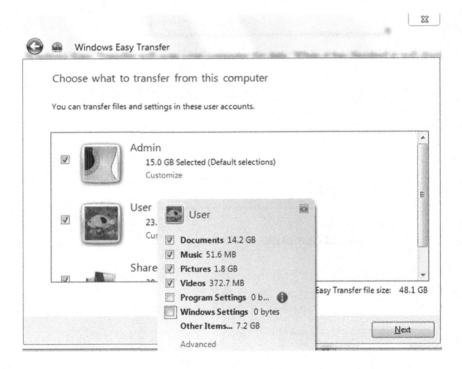

Remove the check mark next to Windows Settings. Click on the little red X button in the upper right hand corner of the above screen. Then click on the **Next** button.

You will be asked for a password to use on your data file. There is no need to enter a password so just click on the **Next** button.

You will now be prompted for a location where you wish to save your data. You should double-click on the drive letter associated with the external drive that is plugged into your computer. Once you double-click on the drive, click on the **Save** button.

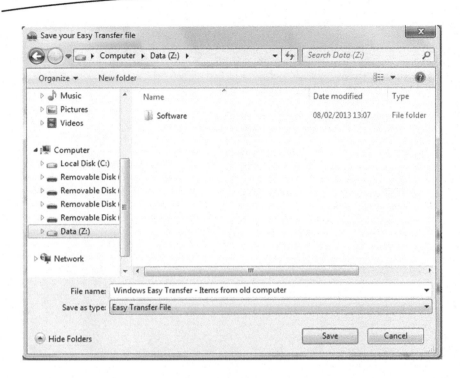

Windows will now start saving your selected data to the external drive. This may take a while so I think it's coffee time while we wait.

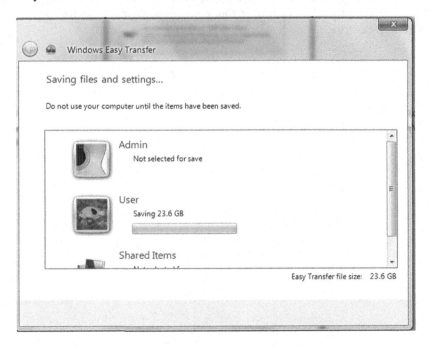

When the data is finished saving, click on **Next** and you will be at the final instruction screen.

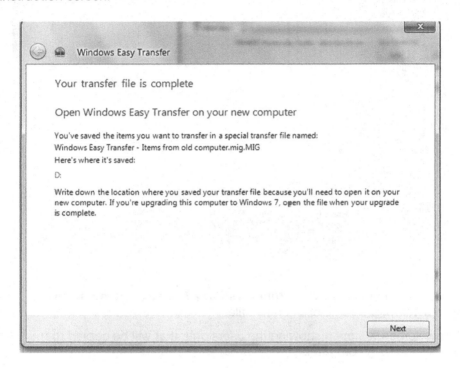

Click on the **Next** button and close the screen. Unplug the external drive.

On your New Computer

Open your desktop from the Start screen, go to your File Explorer – bottom left, and then find your external drive in the drives listed on the left hand pane

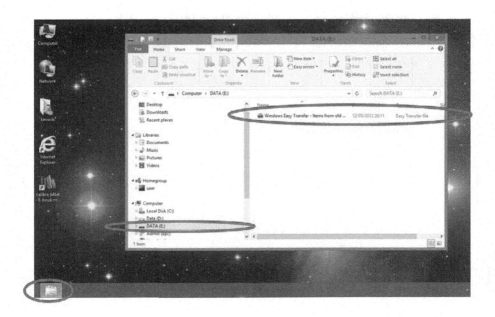

There should be a file called: **Windows Easy Transfer – Items from old computer.mig.** Double click on this file.

A new screen will open showing the users data that will be copied to the new Windows 8 computer.

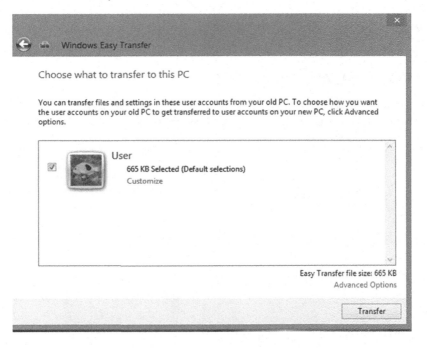

Make sure your user name is checked and click Transfer.

After the data has been transferred, you will be shown a new screen with two options. These options are:

See what was transferred

When you click on this option, Windows Easy Transfer will display a report of all the data and items that were transferred to your new Windows 8 computer.

See a list of apps you might want to install on your new PC

When you click on this option, Windows Easy Transfer will display a report of the applications that were installed on your old computer. You can then use this list to determine if you wish to install any of them again on your new computer.

When you are ready you can then click on the **Close** button to close Windows Easy Transfer.

Your data has now been successfully transferred to your new Windows 8 computer.

Chapter 4

Windows 8

Windows 8/8.1 comes in different forms from tablets to desktop PCs. For this book I will be using a laptop computer and demonstrating common tasks using a point and click installation of Windows 8.

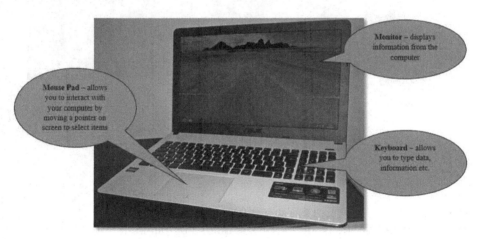

Using the tablet versions of Windows 8 will differ slightly as they are touch screen devices, but more similarly to a Windows 8.1 touch screen on a laptop.

The Start Screen

Once you have logged on you will be greeted with the Start screen.
The Start screen is made up of an arrangement of colorful tiles, each tile
representing an application. You click (or tap) the tile to run the app.

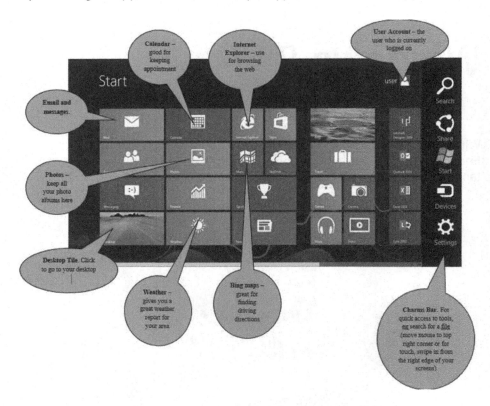

You will notice that the using the tiles is quite a bit different from using the
Desktop (what prior versions of Windows used). The Desktop is still there,
so don't panic. The Start Screen is part of Microsoft's move to make
Windows more similar to phone and tablet interfaces. You will also note
that navigating from the Start Screen can be more challenging than in prior
versions of Windows. There is a way, but it is hidden and we will discuss this
in the Charms section right after we take a look at the Desktop.

The Desktop

The Desktop is your main work area. It's pretty much a representation of your desk at home where you could have letters or photos on your desk. Similarly, Windows Desktop could have documents in Microsoft Word (your letters) or a photo open. Windows Desktop is similar to older versions of Windows and it organizes your files for you in folders (directories). Similarly to Windows, you click on a file to open it in the Desktop.

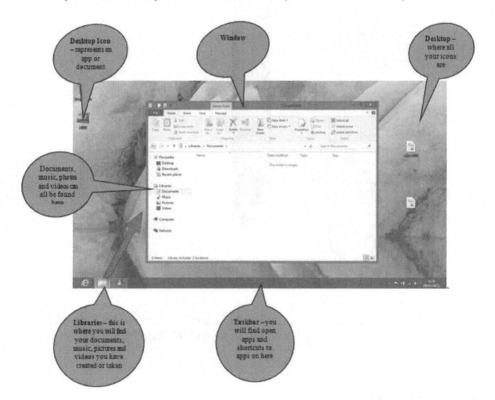

Charms

Charms is a new feature introduced in Windows 8 and continued in 8.1, that gives you access to Search, Share, Start, Devices, and Settings.

Point to, or move the mouse to the upper-right corner of your screen to see the Charms. When the Charms appear, scroll up or down the edge to click the one you want.

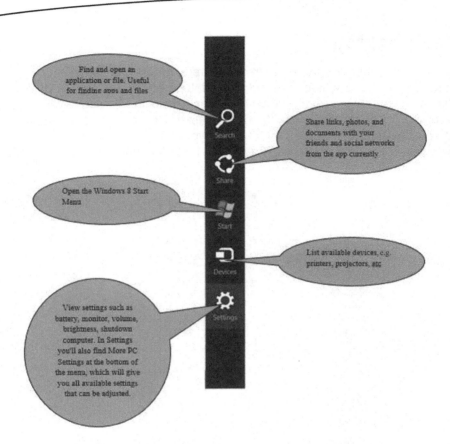

In using the Start Menu you may find that you need, for instance, to find a file and so you would use Search. If you get stuck on one of the tiles on the Start screen, then you can "get out" by opening the Charms and finding what you want.

Hot Corners

Windows 8 makes use of what it calls hotspots. These can be accessed by moving the pointer to various corners of the screen to reveal certain tools. If you get stuck on the Start Screen, these are the hidden options that are available in Windows. You can also reveal Charms on the left but this is not a good idea because of interference with stuff like scroll bars down there. So use the upper right corner.

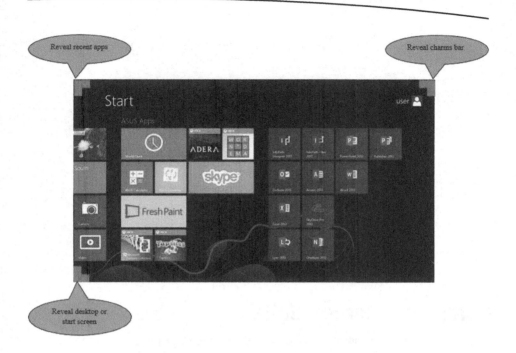

The Taskbar

The task bar at the bottom of your screen by default, shows applications that are currently open (shown by translucent box around icon as can be seen below). It can also be used to pin shortcuts to favorite applications such as Internet Explorer for quick access.

On the right hand side of the taskbar is the area known as the system tray. The system tray contains miniature icons for easy access to system functions such as the printer, volume, clock and any system messages or alerts. Click on an icon to view and access the details and controls. This will vary depending on the open application on your computer as there are hidden icons you can view by clicking on the little triangle.

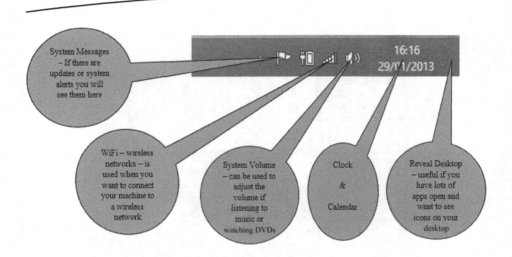

Computer Storage Units

Much like length can be measured in meters or yards, miles or kilometres, or weight in kilograms, computer storage is measured in bytes and kilobytes.

For example, 1 kilobyte is often rounded to 1000 bytes for ease of use.

Without getting too technical, it's exactly 1024 bytes in a kilobyte because computers use **2s** to count (2, 4, 8, 16, 32, etc.), **not 10s** (1, 10, 100, 1000, etc.) like we do.

Bit	All computers work on a numbering system called the binary code, i.e. they process data in ones or zeros. This 1 or 0 is called a bit.
Byte	Consists of 8 bits
Kilo-byte	1024 bytes
Mega-byte	1024 kilo-bytes (1,000,000 bytes)
Giga-byte	1024 mega-bytes (1,000,000,000 bytes)
Tera-byte	1024 giga-bytes (1,000,000,000,000 bytes)

A character in a word document takes up 1 byte, (a character is a single letter, number or symbol e.g., 'A', 'B', 'C', '1', '2', '3', '@', '£', '$', etc.)

Chapter 5

Finding Apps using the Start Window

Finding Applications

Many of the most commonly used applications you have can be found on the Start screen, e.g., Microsoft Word or Internet Explorer.

If you right click on your Start screen, a bar at the bottom pops up, click on 'All Apps' to reveal the apps installed on your computer. Some people have hundreds of apps on their computer. Even on this computer, I have filled a page with this list of apps and already, looking through this to find a file is not a task you want to do lots of times a day. So this can get out of control. So how do you solve that problem?

A quick way to find apps is to activate the Charms bar by moving your mouse to the top right hand corner of the screen. Then in the bar that appears click Search.

You can search 3 categories of things on your computer: Apps such as Word or Media Player, settings such as Disk Defragment or Windows Update and your files such as documents, letters, photos, etc.

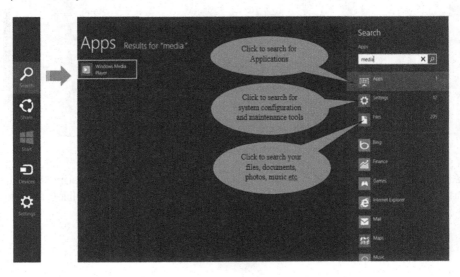

Chapter 6

File Management in Windows

Types of Files

There are many different types of files. There are the files an end user uses, like graphics files, word processing files, video files and so on. These can be accessed and may be changed by the end user and the filenames can be changed as well. However, other files on your system should not have their names changed; they may cause a program not run or may even cause your operating system to fail. There are files that are used by the system that are hidden from end users by default, so that they do not inadvertently mess them up. These can generally be accessed by changing settings on your computer, unless your system administrator has decided not to allow access.

The type of file is usually indicated by a file extension. For example

Photographs and a pictures are often named

Photo_of_tom.**jpg**

Word documents using Microsoft Word usually have an extension of .doc or .docx.

For example, letter_to_mark.**doc**

If these are user files, then you can change the part of the name before the extension, but you should not change the extension.

There are also program files that allow you to run specific applications on your system. These programs often have a bunch of supporting files that also are important for the program to run correctly. Files that run programs on your computer often have the extension .exe and you should not change their name. Supporting files may have the extension .dll or .htm or others, and these definitely should not have their names or their locations changed.

File Naming

End users typically have a large number of files on their computer. All of your pictures, videos, graphic files, pdfs, Microsoft Word or Excel documents are files that you have on your system and they all have a name so that you can identify them. Many of us have thousands of files. Imagine if they all had names like 01.doc, 02.doc. How would you know what is what? Now suppose you are a photographer and you have 10,000 pictures.

When naming files, it is a good idea to give them meaningful names. This helps you find them later either by using the Search function or through browsing through your files. It is better to think this through from the start, so that you have file names that are descriptive and consistent. If you get started on the right foot, you will not be searching for hours later on for that file you need, or worse, reuse the name and overwrite the file and lose it. We will discuss directories later in this chapter, but in a given directory, you cannot have two files with the same name. So if you try to drag and drop a bunch of photos from one computer onto another, and the file names were simply numbers, which is the case in a lot of camera applications, then any file that existed before would be overwritten by a new file with the same name. You could unknowingly wipe out many of your prize photos. Many but not all applications warn you about this, but it is easy to blow through the warning and lose your valuable file. The answer to this problem is better file naming. So start now.

Here are some file naming tips:

- Avoid special characters; some are not allowed and some get changed by applications.

- Don't use spaces. Capitalize the first letter of each word instead. You can use underscores or dashes instead to help readability.

- Use dates for easier search.

- If you can categorize your names, do so. For instance, use LetterFred_123014 if you write a lot of letters.

- Try to use identifying numbers if you have them: If you happen to be a book editor, you might name a chapter 978-1-4842-0806-9-CH06. That is, Chapter 6 in this book (using the ISBN).

- If you are going to use a category over and over, you can abbreviate them. For instance, InvFH_011515 might be an invoice to Fred Hughes with the date.

- If you have more than one version of a file, then you may also want to add a version number to a file name. So, a revision to the chapter above might be 978-1-4842-0806-9-CH06-V02.

  So give this some thought. For example, if you are a lawyer, you might start with client name, then case number, then date. The point is, that if you do not, you WILL lose files; you will waste time looking for them and search only helps so much.

How File Directories Work

Files in Desktop

All of your files can be found in the File Explorer located on your taskbar on your Desktop.

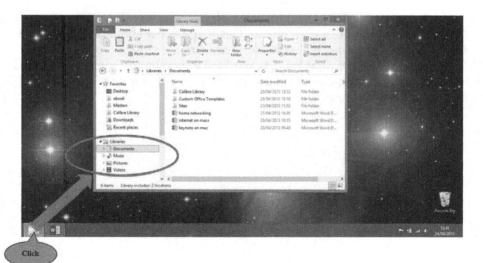

About half way down the left hand pane you'll see a section called 'Libraries'. This is the standard directory structure used in Windows to store your files. The folders (directories) in this area are Music, Pictures and Videos. There are reasons to keep these directories named in this manner. However, as you can see, you can create your own subdirectories under these directories and then subdirectories.... and so on. Note the three subdirectories and the three Word files in the center of the screen. You can click on them to open them.

Note the arrow next to Documents in the figure. This indicates that there are one or more subdirectories. You can click on the arrow and the subdirectories will appear indented under the directory name. It is a very good idea to consider what subdirectories you want to have on your computer and go ahead and set them up. You can always add more, but if you do, you may have to move a lot of files around to fix the new setup. Once, the directories are there, you simply can save files to the appropriate directory using the File/Save commands in your Windows application. Windows applications are set up so that they will show you the directory structure in your File Explorer so that you can choose where to put the file. While you can sort the files by name and date, if you have a pile of files in one directory, it can take a while to find what you want -- which is why file naming is important. In the end, if you could see all the directories and files in your Libraries directory, it would look something like an upside down tree.

Searching for Files

Up to this point we have been focusing on the Desktop. But you can use Charms to conduct a search for your files if you know something about the file name. You can type in your search name; make sure you select Files (as highlighted on the right hand side) to tell Windows to search in your files libraries. The possible candidates appear on the left side of the screen and so you can select from them.

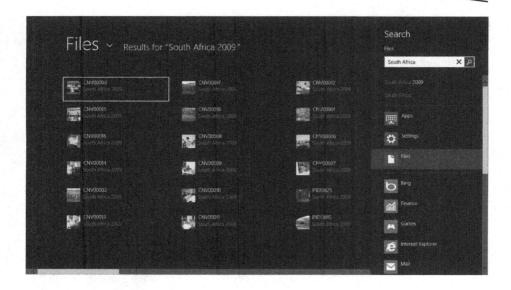

Quick Search the Internet

You can even use the search tool on the Charms bar to search using the Bing search engine. This makes using Windows 8 on a touch screen easier. Having a touch screen is a significant advantage if you are using Windows 8 or 8.1.

Alternatively, you can search using Internet Explorer all from within the Start screen and Charms.

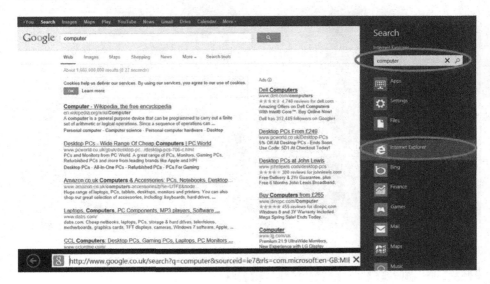

Moving Files

The easiest way to move files is to open your File Explorer then find your file, click and drag it to the new folder as shown below. You can highlight multiple files and drag them to a directory as well. The problem with drag and drop is what if you miss; or mistakenly drag and drop something you did not expect. The stability of the screen in Windows 8 is not the same as in prior versions of Windows and so it is simpler to make mistakes with drag and drop. If you are not careful you may find your Documents directory in your Pictures directory. Alternatively and more safely, you can cut and paste documents from one directory to another.

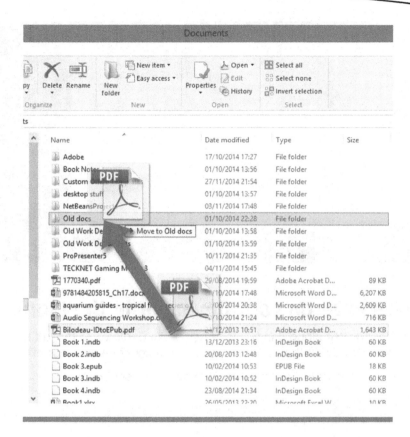

Editing and Deleting Files

You can delete files by clicking on the file in your File Explorer and pressing the Delete key on your keyboard. You can also drag a file, or files, to the trash.

When files are deleted in this way they are actually copied to the trash which means if you accidentally delete a file, you can always restore it by copying it back from the trash folder. Files are permanently deleted if you empty the trash. In Windows the trash is called the Recycle Bin.

Saving Files on your Device or in the Cloud

Saving files to your cloud can be done using File Explorer. In the left hand pane of the window at the top you should see a section called 'OneDrive'

You can click and drag files to the new directory as shown here.

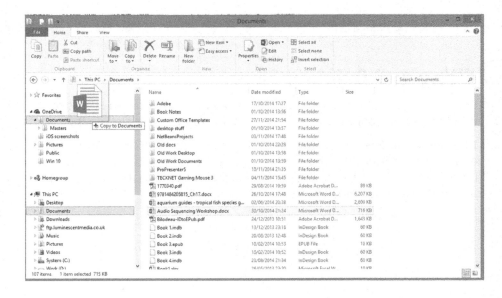

You can also save files directly from an application. For example if you are in Microsoft Word you can save a file directly to your cloud (OneDrive).

How Windows Organizes Files

Windows organizes files into different directories called *libraries*.

Documents

Downloads

Music

Pictures

Videos

Although it doesn't do this automatically. When saving files you should save them in the relevant library. For example, if you are working on Word documents in Microsoft Word then save all your work into the documents library.

Similarly if you are saving photographs off your camera or phone, put them into the Pictures library.

If you are downloading music off Amazon for example, download them to the Music library.

All of your downloads from Internet Explorer or any other web browser can be saved into Downloads. Alternatively, you may want them in the appropriate directory. Be aware that if you save in two different directories that you may get confused with which version of the file is current. This creates the common problem of overwriting the newer version of a file or using an older version when you thought it was the newer one.

7

Using the Internet: Browsers

One of the great joys of having a computer is calling up information from the Internet. In this chapter, we'll look at *browsers*. Browsers are programs that make searching the Internet—also known as the *World Wide Web*—simple. You'll be able to find information on anything, keep up with the news, or watch your favorite dramas.

There are three browsers that most people use to "surf" the web: Internet Explorer, Google Chrome, and Firefox. In general you don't need all three, but it's a good idea to have at least one alternative to Internet Explorer. Some things just work better with one browser rather than another.

First, let's take a quick look at Internet Explorer.

Internet Explorer

Using Internet Explorer as your browser is the easiest choice. It comes with Windows 8.1, so it is already installed on your computer and ready to use. Find the tile on the Start screen with the "swoosh" encircling the lower-case "e" and press or click on it. You will see a screen that looks like this:

Notice the long, narrow box top left that contains the web address of the page you are visiting. Generally, the addresses you'll see, begins with http:// or https://. The term "URL," stands for Uniform Resource Locator and is just another name for web address. In this box, you input the URL and hit Enter to get dropped onto the web page associated with the URL.

When you first open Internet Explorer, it will take you to MSN.com, Microsoft's news and entertainment web site. To see how easy it is to go from site to site, type in www.apress.com or simply apress.com (don't worry about the http://). The screen below will pop up.

In addition to the address box there is another long, narrow box that says "bing". Bing is Microsoft's **search engine**—the technology that searches the web for any terms or phrases that you type into that box. Just for fun, type in anything that interests you right now. It might be the name of your favorite TV show, a hobby, the name of a high school friend, or just about anything.

You can even bypass the "official" search box and enter your search term in the address box. You can also switch from Bing to Google Search or other search engines if you wish.

There are many more features of Internet Explorer. You will learn about some of them in the next chapter, but you will also learn by playing around with the program. You can't "break" Internet Explorer, so don't be afraid to push buttons or change any of the settings. You can always restore things to the way they were.

Features Common to Most Web Browsers

Before we discuss Chrome and Firefox, let's take a step back and look at some of the features you'll find in all three browsers. Each, you'll find, works in much the same way. All of the items discussed here can be found near the top of the screen, with most of them in the upper right.

Navigation arrows. In the upper left-hand corner of the screen you'll find arrows. Once you start "browsing"—going from web site to web site—you can use the arrows to move backward or forward through the sites you have visited. If you've typed in a search term and visited a few pages, hit the back button as many times as you must to get back to the original page. That will give you a feel for its use.

Bookmarks. In Internet Explorer, look around the Bing search box. You'll see a *icons*, which are tiny representations of web sites (like MSN), the Facebook "like" thumb, games you can play, local weather, and more. Chrome and Firefox each have a similar *bookmarks bar*, and you can customize each to display the sites you visit regularly, or those you simply want to remember. Doing so will make it much easier to find the web sites you like and use the most.

Closing program, minimizing, or resizing. Now look at the top right of the screen in any browser. You'll see a red "X," which will close the program and return you to the start screen. The horizontal bar will "minimize" the screen, which means it will make it disappear until you wish to recall it by tapping on the Explorer icon at the bottom of the screen. The small rectangle allows you to "size" the screen to any shape or size you want. This is sometimes helpful if you have two programs you want to see at the same time.

Home. Just below those items in Internet Explorer and Firefox you'll see an image of a house. (In Chrome, it's on the left side of the screen.) Clicking or tapping on this button will bring you to your *Home page*, the page you will also see whenever you open your browser. In Internet Explorer, it's automatically set for msn.com, as mentioned, but you can change it to anything you like. (See Settings, below. That option, in any browser, allows you to change the home page.)

Favorites. Near the top on the right side of each browser is a star. This is the universal icon that lets you save your *favorites*. Favorites, also called *bookmarks*, make it easy to go back to the web sites you visit often. When you find a site you want to remember, click or tap the star, and then "Add to favorites." That will save the web address for you, either in a special folder or list, or on the bookmarks bar mentioned above.

History. If you're in Internet Explorer right now, go ahead and tap on the star right now. You'll see three "tabs." The first says Favorites, and it will eventually contain a list of all your favorite sites. Don't worry about the middle one, Feeds, but click on **History**. That keeps a record of where you have been in the World Wide Web. Among other reasons, it's useful if you forgot to bookmark a site and want to go back again. Each of the browsers has a history feature, though in Firefox and Chrome, you access them through the settings feature. You can set your browser to erase History if you prefer.

Settings. In Internet Explorer, you'll see an image of a gear. This is a symbol for *settings*. In the other browsers, the icon of choice consists of three stacked horizontal lines (indicating a menu). Click or tap that image now in any browser and you'll find some handy features. As you can see, you can print the page you're looking at (great for things like airplane tickets), or you can save it as a file you can call up whenever you'd like or you can "zoom" the page—make it bigger or smaller. You'll use this feature a lot, by the way, since many designers of web pages seem to like tiny type.

Security. In Internet Explorer, choose Internet Options from the Settings menu. Click on the Security tab. There, you can set the security level that makes you comfortable. That will help you avoid the "bad guys" on the web who work hard to trick you into parting with your money or information. It can also limit the kind of images you see. All browsers have a similar security feature.

Refresh. Each browser, somewhere near the address box, sports a circle made out of an arrow. This is the *refresh* button. The page you are looking at will "reload" when you tap that button, giving you the latest version. This can be helpful if, for example, you looked at a weather site an hour ago, and you want to update the weather report.

Tabs. One last thing before we move on. At the top of the screen in each browser, you'll see a second, shadowy tab. Click on that, and voila—a new screen appears. You can have many screens going at the same time.

Google Chrome

While the majority of people use a version of Internet Explorer to surf the web, many prefer Google's browser, called Chrome. One reason is that many people think the Google search engine is better than the Bing search engine. Others like its "stripped down" feel compared to Internet Explorer. Finally, some people think Chrome is "safer," because hackers—the bad guys—spend more time finding vulnerabilities in Internet Explorer than in Chrome.

Here is the opening screen for Chrome. Note that besides the search box front and center, it shows the sites you visit the most. Click or tap on any one, and you're transported there instantly.

One important thing: Chrome did not come with your Windows 8.1 computer automatically. You have to download it. That means going to a specific web address to install it on your computer. This is very easy to do.

To get Chrome, type www.google.com/chrome/ into the web address bar. Or you can simply type "Chrome" into the Bing search bar and then click on the first link at the top of the list that appears. Then choose "Download" at the top of the screen and then the blue "Download Chrome" bar in the middle of the page. Follow the directions. (You'll need to agree to the terms. Most people simply check the box and proceed.)

Once you have loaded Chrome onto your computer, you can find it in your Desktop if it is not loaded on your Start menu. Once you have opened the program and are looking at the Start screen, you'll notice something important: It is set up much like Internet Explorer. You have the arrows top left, the address box next to them, and the bookmarks bar below.

Play around with Chrome to understand how to use it best.

Mozilla Firefox

Your third option for a browser is Mozilla Firefox. Internet Explorer is an excellent browser, as is Chrome. Why would anyone want Firefox? Well, it too is an excellent browser, plus it has a reputation for being less "buggy," meaning it won't stop working for no apparent reason. (Well, at least not as often as Internet Explorer does.) It's also considered the "safest" of the three browsers.

Like Chrome, you won't find Firefox on your computer. You have to install it. To do that, type this into the address bar of your current browser: https://www.mozilla.org/en-US/firefox/new/. You can also simply type "Firefox" in the search box and then choose one of the options. Once you do, tap or click on "Free Download" and follow the instructions. Doing so may immediately download an installation program. If that's the case, a box will appear in Internet Explorer asking if you want to run the program. Choose Run. In Chrome, that same file will appear, but in a slightly different format in the lower left corner.

Once you have installed Firefox, open it up by looking on your Desktop or Start menu.

Again, you'll notice that the screen elements are familiar. You have the star for favorites, the house to access your Home page, and the three horizontal bars where you can choose your settings. There is also a list icon to the right of the star, which will show all your bookmarks on the left side of the screen.

Firefox also offers a big search box near the top. Its search engine is provided by Yahoo!, another big Internet company that offers many services you might find valuable. But under Settings, you can change the search engine to Google, Bing, or anything else you'd like.

Summary

You have three excellent choices for browsing, or surfing, the World Wide Web: Internet Explorer, Chrome, and Firefox. Any of them will do a fine job for you and give you the power to answer any question you might have, present the news, provide entertainment, and in general help you enjoy life more. Next let's do a little hands-on work with Internet Explorer.

Chapter 8

Using Internet Explorer

As with other applications in Windows 8 there are two ways of accessing Internet Explorer in Windows 8.1. One is to use the Desktop tile and access it similarly to prior versions of Windows from the menu. The other is to use the Internet Explorer tile circled below. We will focus on using Internet Explorer from this icon as it saves you at least one step. So, on your Start screen click on Internet Explorer.

In the address bar below type the name of the thing you are looking for. For example, I'm looking for the Amazon website. So I will type Amazon into the address bar. Note that the address bar acts as not only a place to insert the URL of a website (like Amazon.com) but also allows for searches on Amazon.

As you start to type, Internet Explorer will try to find the website. You can see below that Internet Explorer has found Amazon's website. Just click or tap on the result and it will take you to the website. Note that your screen may look somewhat different from this one, but will have the same options.

Adding a Site to Favorites

To add the site to favorites, click the drawing pin shown below or alternatively you might see a 5 point star on newer versions of Internet Explorer, which will allow you to add a favorite site to your Favorites list.

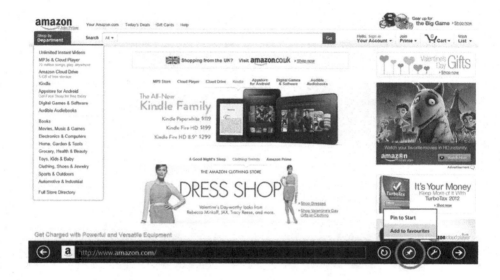

Then click Add to favorites.

Chapter 9

Using Email

When you first set up an account in Windows 8 you'll be offered the chance to log in with your Windows Live ID. If you don't have one, it's worth setting one up as discussed in Chapter 13.

This chapter starts with a look at what a basic email system looks like using Hotmail as the browser. It then goes on to show how to set up one or more of your email accounts on your device. In doing so, you will be able to click on your email icon and open up your email without going first to the browser and typing it in. If you are using Outlook on Exchange for instance, the benefit of having your email set up on the device, rather than accessing it through a browser is significant.

Let's start with a look at our existing Hotmail account. From the Start screen, click on the Mail icon (tile).

The left pane shows your account's Inbox, Drafts, Sent Items, etc.

The center pane shows a list of messages corresponding to the box selected in the left hand pane.

The right pane displays the email message highlighted in the center pane.

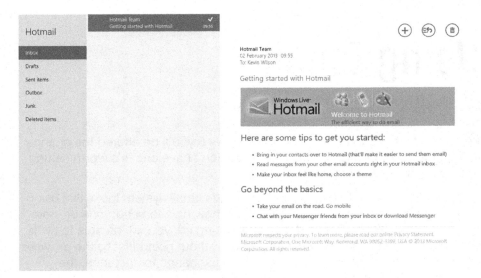

If you want to add other email accounts, perhaps you have a Gmail or Yahoo mail account, you can add a new account with the Settings charm. As discussed before, you can sweep a finger inward from the right side of the screen, or you can move the mouse pointer to the top right corner of the screen, to get the Charms to appear as shown below. Then choose the Settings option.

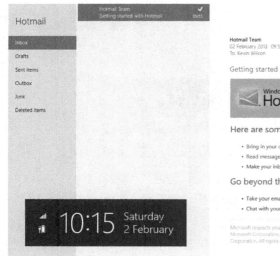
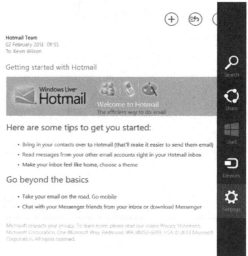

Then choose Accounts from the Settings menu.

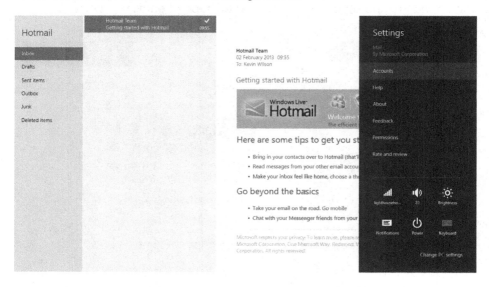

A new pane will appear. Click *Add an account* and enter the details for a new email account.

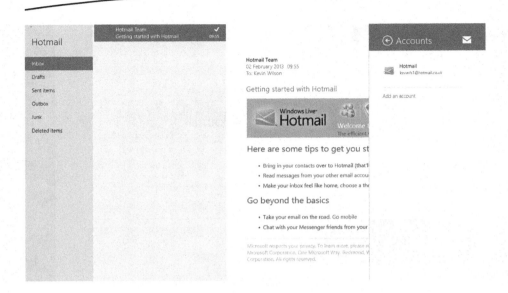

Pick the account type. You can choose between Hotmail, Google, Yahoo and Exchange and others depending on the type of email you want.

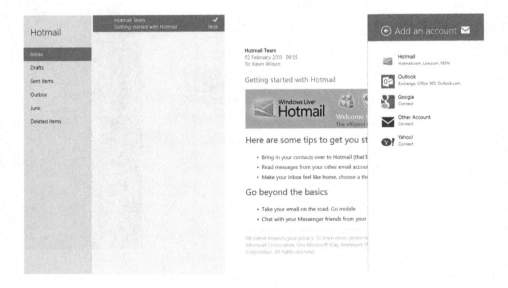

You then enter your email address and the password for the account you want to add, and choose Connect. You can repeat this process to add your other accounts.

Chapter 10

Sending an Email

If you use the Mail app in Windows 8.1, it is somewhat different from prior versions of Windows. This can be confusing to new users. Note that you can run your email off of File Explorer by clicking on the Desktop icon and finding your email program in the menu; a more traditional look and feel that will be familiar to anyone who has used Windows before. However, if you are using the Mail app on the Start menu, as in Chapter 9, this section shows you how to use Hotmail in Windows 8.1.

To create and send a new email message click the *Send new message* icon (+).

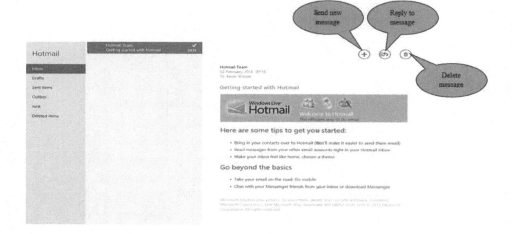

Fill in the email address, and type your message. Once you are done click send message.

Note that there are also icons for replying to an existing message or deleting a message (trash can).

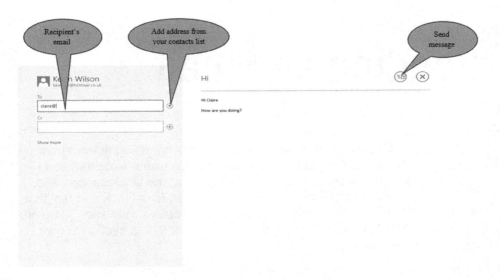

11

Scanning Documents

By default, Windows uses 'Windows Fax and Scan' to scan documents. There are other apps available that are bundled with scanners and available for purchase, but for simplicity I am going to use 'Windows Fax and Scan'. To get started, activate the Charms bar, go to search and type 'scan'.

Click 'Windows Fax and Scan' and you should see the main screen

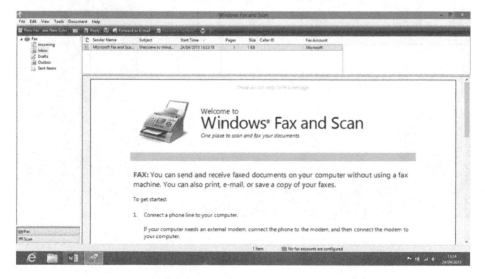

Plug your scanner in, if this is the first time Windows 8 has tried to install it.

If it fails to install, run the software that comes with the scanner; see their website for more information.

To scan a document click New Scan.

You will find all of your scans in your 'Scanned Documents' folder in your Documents library. This can be accessed from your desktop using the Desktop tile.

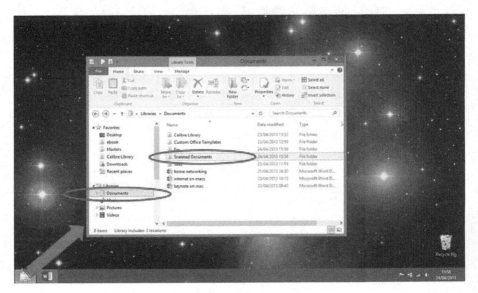

Chapter **12**

Printing Documents

Printing from Windows 8 apps can be a little different from prior versions of Windows. If you are working in the desktop in Windows 8 or 8.1, and are printing documents in say Word or any other traditional application, then printing document is quite similar to older versions of Windows. You simply click on a print icon, or if there is not one, then click on File, then select Print, and you then can select your printer, or choose to save the document to your computer as a file in PDF format, or use the other options that you have listed on the screen.

However, if you are in a Windows 8 app, using a tile on your Start screen, it's a little different. If you are in a Windows 8 app, then there is no visible option for printing, and if you try right clicking, there still is not. In this example, I want to print a web page from Internet Explorer having gone into Internet Explorer from the tile on the Start screen. In order to print, you need to activate the Charms bar by moving your mouse pointer to the top right corner of the screen and once in the Charms bar, select Devices.

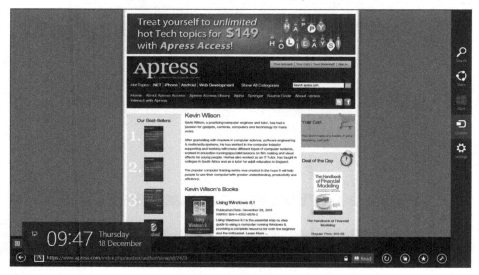

You can now select your printer from the list, clicking on the printer option of your choice.

A settings screen for your printer appears, where you can change the number of copies, orientation, color mode, and other settings.

Click on the Print button to print.

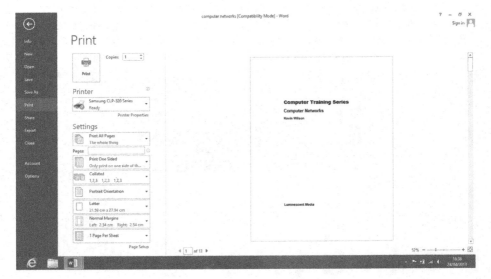

Chapter 13

Creating a Microsoft Account

A Microsoft Account is an email address and a password that you use in Windows 8.1 enabling you to access OneDrive, Outlook.com, the family safety options (that will be discussed in Chapter 24), Xbox Live, a Windows Phone, Office 365, your email directly, and more. You can use the same account for all of your Microsoft Windows devices. The bottom line is that you want to create a Microsoft account.

It is wise to enter the email address you use for the things you use the most. It is likely you will give priority to your favorite email account (Windows Live, Yahoo, Gmail, Hotmail, etc.), but perhaps to the one used for your social networking sites. It is not necessary to have a Windows Live email address. However, if you wish, you can create an email address for this purpose (for instance, if you do not have one already).

To sign up for a Microsoft account, open your web browser and go to:

signup.live.com

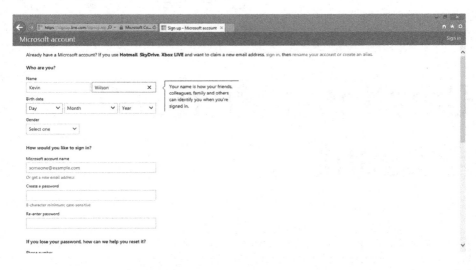

Fill in the form and click accept

Set Up a Microsoft Account on your PC

If you don't have a Microsoft account email address, you must create a new one – see previous section.

If you do not have an active Microsoft account, you can activate it using the following procedure. First, activate the Charms menu by moving your mouse to the top right corner, then click Settings, then tap or click Change PC settings.

In the left pane, tap or click Users. Then tap or click *Switch to a Microsoft account*.

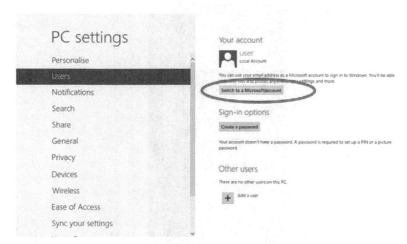

Enter a password, and click on Next.

In the *Sign in with a Microsoft account* dialog box, type in your Windows Live ID, Gmail, Yahoo or Hotmail email address you used when you created your Microsoft account, and then click on Next.

Enter the security info (you don't necessarily need a phone number and you can use your same email if you don't have an alternative) and then click Finish.

Adding a New User

You may want others to use your device. For instance, your children. If so, it is a very good idea to set them up as additional users on your computer. You can then set/limit their access to content and rights on the computer as described later on in this book. If you wish to do so, on the Start screen activate the Charms bar and select Settings.

From the Settings charm, select *Change PC settings*.

Select Users, then click *Add a user.*

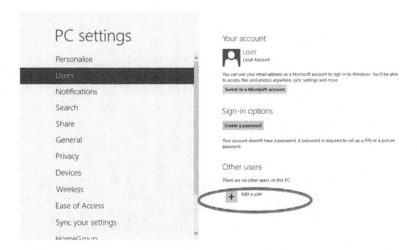

Fill in the new email address form, enter the password you want and the other details including whether or not it's a child's account. This allows you to use Windows 8's Family Safety features (discussed in Chapter 24). Click Next.

On the security info page, add a phone number (optional at time of writing), alternative email address and a security question. This information is kept private and you will only ever be asked this information should you ever forget your password. Click Next.

Add your date of birth and gender (again this info is kept private and is only used to verify your identity), and click the Next button.

Finally, type the random characters displayed on the screen. This is done to stop internet robots from automatically creating email accounts and sending out unsolicited email. Click Next.

Once the account is confirmed, click Finish.

Chapter 14

Using Microsoft App Store

The app store allows you to download and install apps. The app store has both free and paid apps. You can start the app store by clicking or tapping the tile on the Start screen.

Once the store opens, you can browse through the top paid apps, top free apps, or new releases or if you are searching for a specific app activate your Charms bar and select search

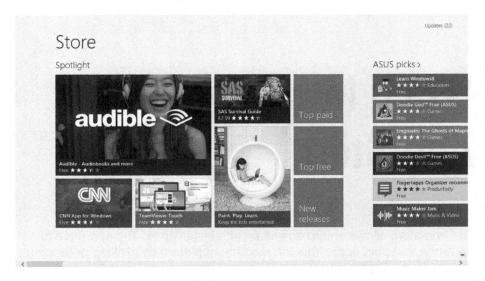

Select Search:

On the search screen, enter a word describing the type of app you are looking for. In this example, I am looking for graphics apps to edit my photographs.

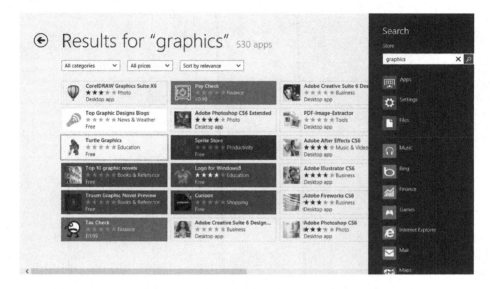

To download or purchase any apps just click or tap on them and follow the download instructions on screen.

Chapter 15

OneDrive

OneDrive is a "cloud" based, file hosting service. OneDrive allows users to access their files from a web browser after uploading them to cloud storage. Users can keep the files private, share them with friends, or make the files public. Publicly shared files do not require a Microsoft account for access. There are several benefits to saving your files in the cloud. The two biggest are probably that OneDrive files are backed up and so you don't have to worry about that and the other is that they do not take up all that space on your device.

To access your OneDrive in a web browser go to onedrive.live.com.

Once logged on you can access documents, pictures and your public area.

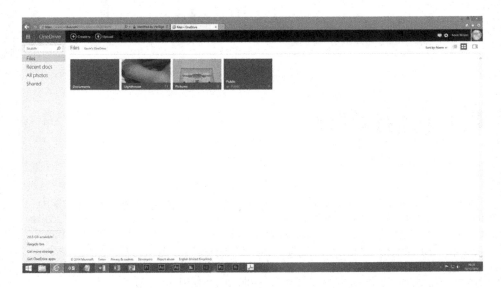

In your documents area, you can actually use a web based version of Microsoft Word 2013 to edit your document and save it back to your OneDrive.

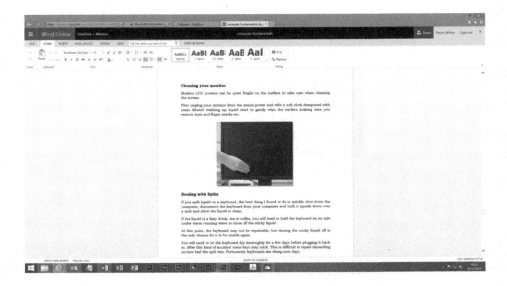

If you are using Windows 8, you can access these files and upload others to OneDrive by using the OneDrive App on your Start screen.

By clicking in the documents section you will find your files.

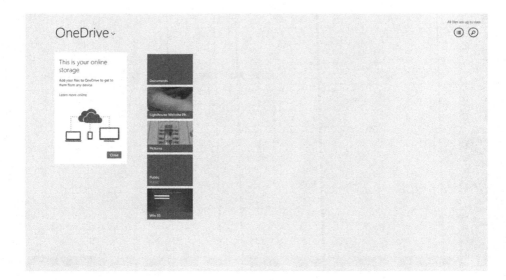

You can open them up and OneDrive will load them directly into your installation of Microsoft Word 2013.

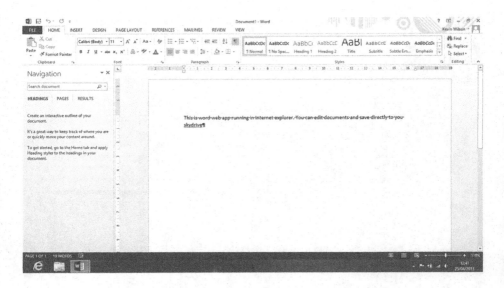

If Word asks you to log in, enter your Microsoft Account email address and password.

Saving onto your OneDrive is the same as if you were saving the file to your computer. Just select your OneDrive from the options in the Save As screen in Office.

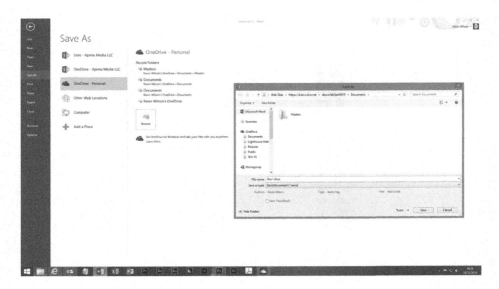

Chapter 16

Organizing your Music

The Music app links in with your Windows account so you can buy any albums or tracks you want through their store Xbox Music.

The Music app also automatically scans your computer for any music and adds it to your library.

Buying Songs and Albums

You can buy songs or albums by your favorite artist right from the Music app.

From in the music app, tap or click the Search charm.

In the Search charm you can search for specific songs, albums, or artists. Now type the name of the song or artist in the search and press Enter.

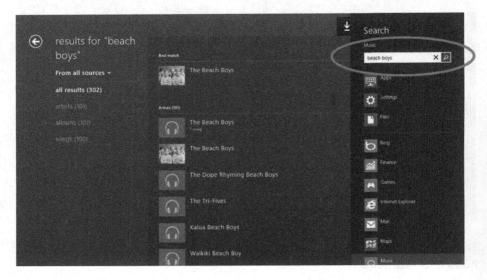

Pick a song or album, and then follow the on-screen instructions to buy it.

Copy Songs from a CD to your PC

If you want to copy music from a CD onto your computer, you can use Windows Media Player. Media Player enables you to rip the files off the disc and encode them to mp3, wma or whatever is required.

To do so:

Open the Search charm.

Enter Windows Media Player into the search, and click on Windows Media Player in the results area circled below.

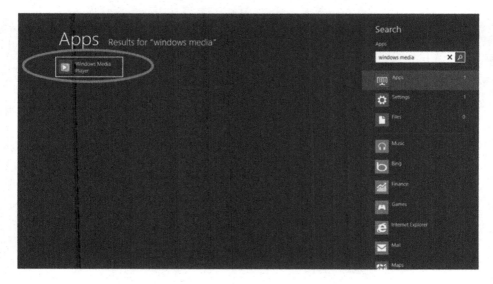

Next, insert an audio CD into the CD drive. Check the boxes next to the songs you want to rip, and then click Rip CD.

When your songs have been copied, you can find and play them in the Music app.

Chapter 17

Videos & DVDs

You can watch movies, TV programs and videos on your computer or phone. Some are free and some are paid. You can buy movies or rent them and have them streamed directly to your computer.

To go to the Movie store, click Video on the Start screen to access Xbox Video which is where Microsoft tries to sell you video.

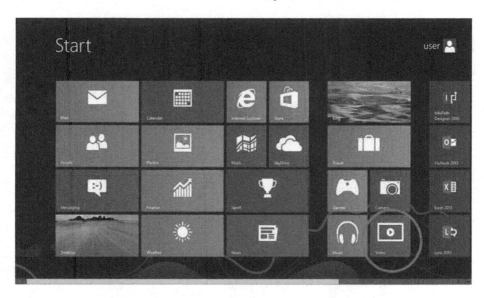

You can browse the store or search for a specific genre or movie/TV title. To do so, activate your Charms bar and select search and type it in.

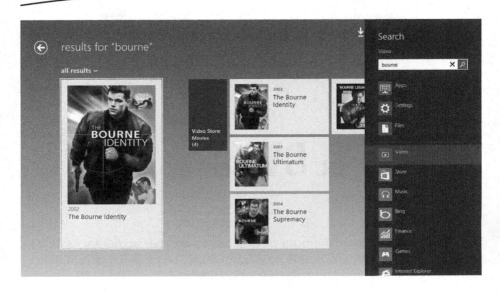

To buy or watch them, just click on the image and follow the instructions on how to complete the download.

Playing DVDs

If you like watching DVDs on your PC, Windows 8 can't play DVD videos out of the box. You have to download a free player. VLC media player plays back CDs, DVDs and other file types.

Just go to their website, `www.videolan.org`, and click download.

When prompted with your download, click run and follow the instructions.

Burning CD/DVDs

In Windows 8.1 you have three disc options:

- Audio CD: Providing 80 minutes of music only but is playable on almost any player.

- Data CD: You can put other file types on it and it will work on a computer, but other devices must support the other file formats.

- Data DVD: You can put over 50 hours of music on it but the device must support WMA, MP3, JPEG, if you have them on the DVD.

To burn it you need to first insert a blank DVD or CD and select

Once you have set up your disk, you need to drag the files and folders you want to burn to the disk to the DVD drive in your Explorer window.

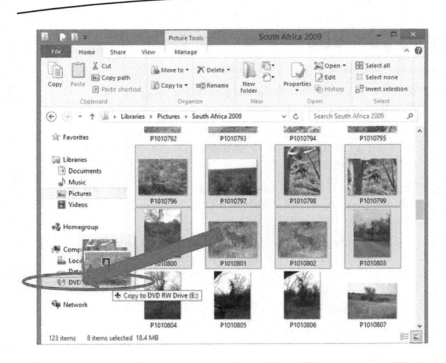

To burn the data to the disk, right click on the DVD drive in the Explorer window and select 'burn to disc' from the menu.

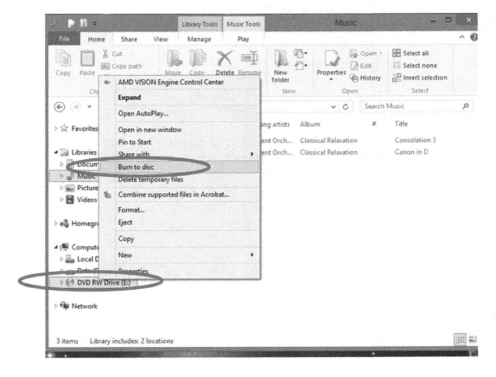

Burning Audio CDs

Burning audio CDs can be done from Windows Media Player. From the Charms bar go to the Search charm and type 'media'.

Once in Media Player, click on the burn tab. You can now click and drag tracks to the burn tab to create a playlist.

Once your disk is full or you have the number of tracks you want, click 'Start burn' to create your CD.

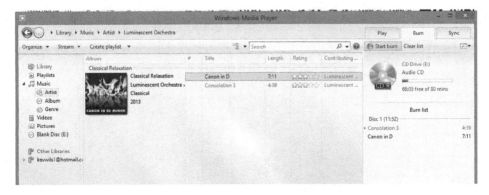

Chapter 18

Uploading from Digital Cameras

Again, you could use the Desktop to do this like you would in prior versions of Windows and the processes are pretty similar, but it is simplest to work from the Start Screen. To get started, plug in your camera using the USB cable. As soon as you plug in for the first time, a message will appear on the top right of the screen asking you what to do with the device you have just plugged in. Click on it.

Once you click on it, click *Import photos and videos*.

> **Note** You will only have to do this the first time you plug your camera into your computer. When you plug your camera in again you will go straight to the photo app.

Select the photos you want by clicking on them, type in the name of the album you want to group your photos in. For instance, this could be a wedding or birthday. Then click import.

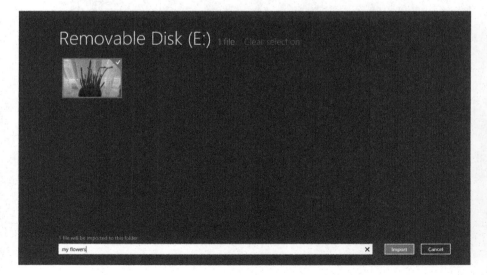

Once you are done importing, click open folder. Here you will be able to see the photos you just imported.

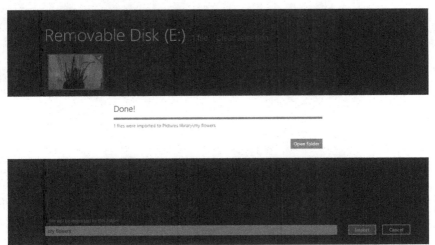

To access your photos at any time, click on the photos app on the Start screen.

19

Connecting to Other Screens or Projectors

There are several applications of utilizing more than one screen. Most people in a work environment can be more productive if they have two screens to work with. This book was edited working with two screens. Projecting the image on your computer onto a screen for a presentation is another common use. Let's get started. Open the Charms bar, select the Devices charm and, then *Second screen.*

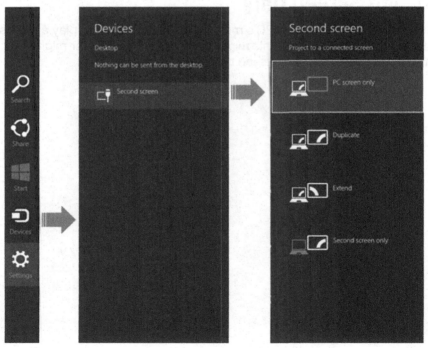

As you can see, there are four options, in the menu in the figure, for handling the screens that are useful under different circumstances.

PC Screen Only

This is the mode used when a screen or projector is attached and the information is to be seen only on the PC's monitor.

Duplicate

What is on the monitor is on the second screen. This is the case in presentations or where you want to have people seeing the same information without having them crowd around a single desktop.

Extend

In this mode the additional screen can to allow you more real estate to put up additional documents. One screen might have the document being worked on while another might be used for looking up supporting materials.

Second Screen Only

This is the case where your PC's monitor is blank and the display appears only on the remote screen. This might be because a presenter might not want to see something to be seen by someone passing by.

Chapter 20

Keyboard Shortcuts

The design of Windows 8 creates some productivity challenges for its users in its attempt to satisfy tablet users while attempting to keep desktop users who were getting their job done with prior versions of Windows. As a result, Windows 8 is significantly easier to use if you happen to have a touch screen, but only a tiny fraction of PC users have them now. Even with touch screens, the chance of creating errors is greatly increased by the interface. Fortunately, keyboard shortcuts make it bit easier to navigate without a touch screen and help reduce mistaken gestures. Here is a list of keyboard short cuts that can help you increase your productivity. But first, two highly useful examples.

To close an app, hold down Alt and press F4.

To get back to the Start screen, press the Windows key. Some common shortcuts to keep in mind:

Keyboard shortcut	Function
⊞ + start typing	Search your PC
Ctrl plus ("+") or Ctrl minus ("-")	Zoom in or out of a large number of items
Ctrl + Scroll wheel	Zoom in or out of a large number of items
⊞ + C	Open the charms menu
⊞ + F	Open the Search charm to search files
⊞ + H	Open the Share charm
⊞ + I	Open the Settings charm
⊞ + J	Switch the main app and snapped app
⊞ + K	Open the Devices charm
⊞ + O	Lock the screen orientation
⊞ + Q	Open the Search charm to search apps
⊞ + W	Open the Search charm to search settings
⊞ + Z	Show the commands available in the app
⊞ + spacebar	Switch input language and keyboard layout
⊞ + Ctrl + spacebar	Change to previously selected input
⊞ + Tab	Cycle through open apps
⊞ + Ctrl + Tab	Cycle through open apps and snap them as they are cycled
⊞ + Shift + Tab	Cycle through open apps in reverse order
⊞ + Pg Up	Move the Start screen and apps to the monitor on the left
⊞ + Pg Dn	Move the Start screen and apps to the monitor on the right
⊞ + Shift + Period (".")	Snaps apps to the left
⊞ + Period (".")	Snaps apps to the right
Esc	Stop or exit the current task
⊞ + L	Lock your PC or switch users
⊞ + M	Minimize all windows
⊞ + Shift + M	Restore minimized windows on the desktop
⊞ + P	Choose a presentation display mood
⊞ + R	Open the Run dialogue box
⊞ + T	Cycle through apps on the taskbar
⊞ + V	Cycle through notifications

⊞ + Shift + V	Cycle through notifications in reverse order
⊞ + X	Open the Quick Link menu
⊞ + F1	Open Windows Help and Support
⊞ + Up arrow	Maximize the desktop window
⊞ + Down arrow	Minimize the desktop window
⊞ + plus ("+") or minus ("-")	Zoom in or out using Magnifier
Alt + F4	Close the active item, or exit the active app
Alt + Enter	Display properties for the selected item
Control + C	Copy the selected item
Control + X	Cut the selected item
Control + V	Paste the selected item
Control + Y	Redo an action
Control + Z	Undo an action
F1	Display Help
F2	Rename the selected item
F3	Search for a file or folder
F4	Display the address bar list in the File Explorer
F5	Refresh the active window
F10	Activate the menu bar in the active app

Chapter 21

Frequently Used Applications

Windows 8.1 comes with a number of pre-installed apps to make life simpler for the user. They are not only useful, but serve to teach people how apps in Windows 8.1 work. We will explore two of them to give you a sense of them so that you can go to the Store and pick out more that suit your needs.

Maps

You can find Maps on the Start screen, or you can activate the Charms bar and select Search. In the search, type in MAPS or select it. Then you can search for any location.

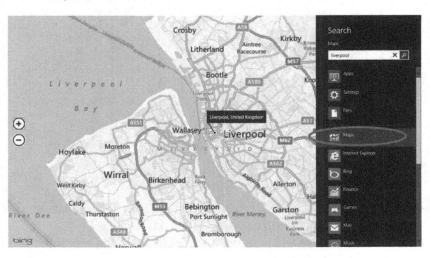

Right click on the map to reveal additional options. On map style you can select a street map (Road view) or satellite map (aerial view). I find Aerial view more descriptive when finding directions.

Right click on the map and select Directions.

Enter your current location and destination.

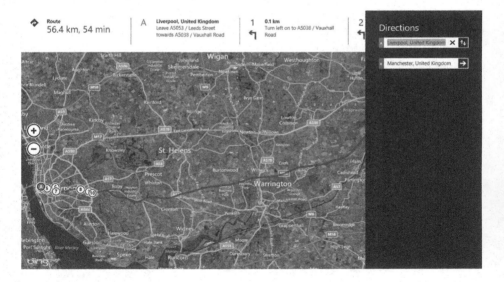

Hit Enter and Bing maps will bring up a route shown at the top of the screen and indicated by a blue line on the map.

Calendar

To access Calendar, click on it from the Start menu.

Once calendar has started it will show you the current month, it also shows public holidays. If you use the same Microsoft account to log in to Calendar as you use for Outlook 2013 and the Mail app, then they can sync up.

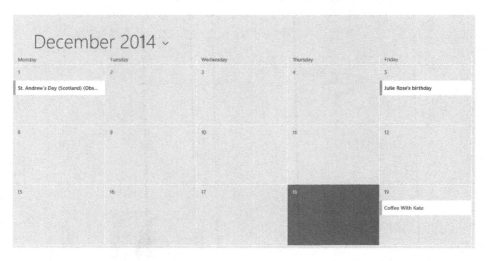

To add an appointment double click on the day in the month and fill in the fields as shown below. Then click save when done.

To move to the previous or next month move your pointer over to the top left or right to reveal the arrows next to the month.

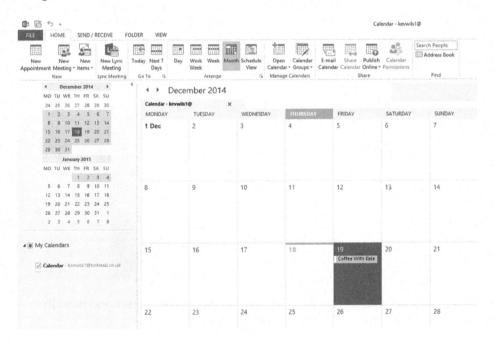

Chapter **22**

Word 2013

Starting Word

Microsoft Word allows you to create many different types of document, from letters, CVs to greetings cards, posters and more.

To launch Word go to the Start menu and select "Word 2013". Alternatively, as you probably already knew, you can access word from the Explorer in the Desktop.

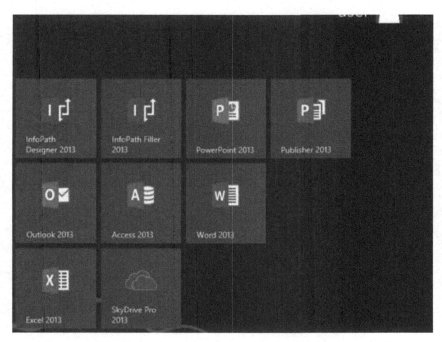

Once Word has loaded, you can select a document from a wide variety of templates, e.g. brochures, CVs, letters, flyers, etc. If you want to create your own, just select Blank. Your recently saved documents are shown on the blue pane on the left hand side.

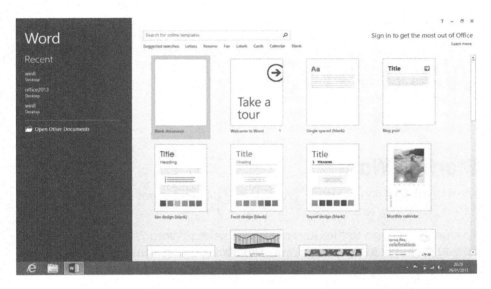

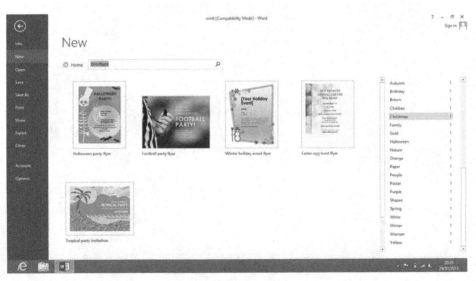

Once you select a template, you will see your main work screen.

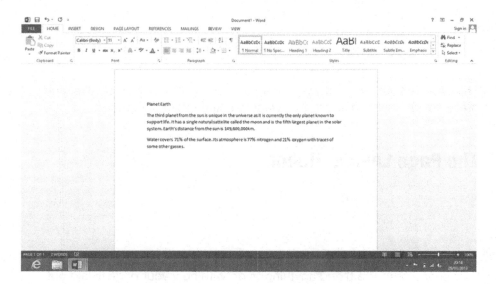

The Ribbon

All the tools used in Microsoft Word are organized into ribbons loosely based on their function.

The most used ribbons are Home, Insert and Page Layout. For normal use of Word these are the ones you will be looking in the most.

The Home Ribbon

You will find your text formatting tools here for making text bold, changing styles, font, paragraph alignment, etc.

The Insert Ribbon

This is where you will find your clipart, tables, pictures, page breaks, and pretty much anything you would want to insert into a document.

The Page Layout Ribbon

This ribbon you will find your page sizes, margins, page orientation (landscape or portrait) and anything to do with how your page is laid out.

Basic text formatting

At the moment our document looks very plain. We need to format it.

To format the document we are going to use the formatting tools. These are on the home ribbon shown below.

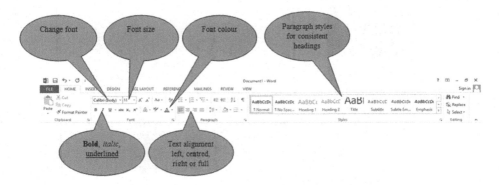

We can change the font, the size of the text, whether it is **bold** or *italic* or underlined.

We can change the alignment of the text whether its

Left aligned

Centered

Right aligned

Or whether the text is fully justified, which means it's aligned with both the left and right margins at the same time as shown in this example. It only really works on paragraphs like this so you can see the left and right margins are both in line.

We can even change the color of the text, maybe a bright red? Or perhaps a nice blue?

So, to format your document we are going to use the predefined styles.

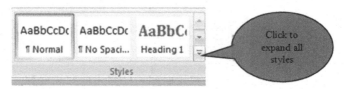

These are styles that have been already created to allow you to keep consistent looking headings and text effects in your documents. They make it easier to apply different font styles and sizes without having to set each individually every time.

So to change the text "Planet Earth" to Title style, highlight the title in your document as shown below.

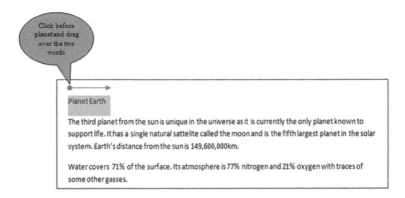

Next, go up to styles in your Home ribbon, and then click title in the styles as shown below.

If I want to change the last paragraph to **bold**, I can select the whole paragraph and click the **bold** button on the home ribbon.

Adding Images

Adding images to your document is easy.

- You can use your own photos and pictures.

- You can use Clipart. Clipart is generally from large libraries of images that can be used in your documents.

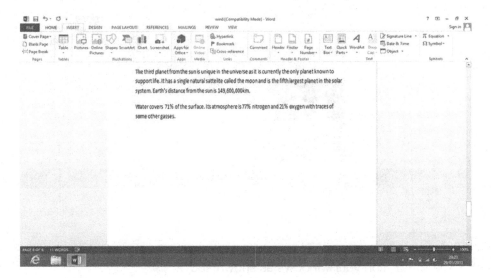

The easiest way to add your own photographs or pictures is to find them in your Explorer window and drag them on top of your document.

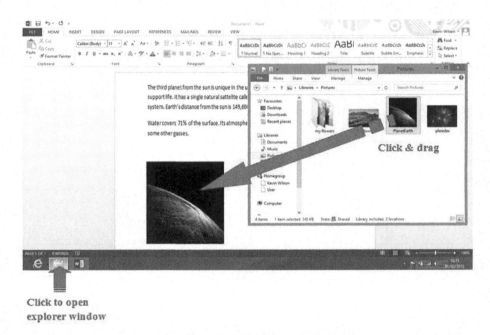

Click to open
explorer window

It helps to position your windows as shown above.

Chapter 23

PowerPoint 2013

Starting PowerPoint

Microsoft PowerPoint allows you to create multimedia presentations. To launch PowerPoint go to the Start screen and tap PowerPoint 2013.

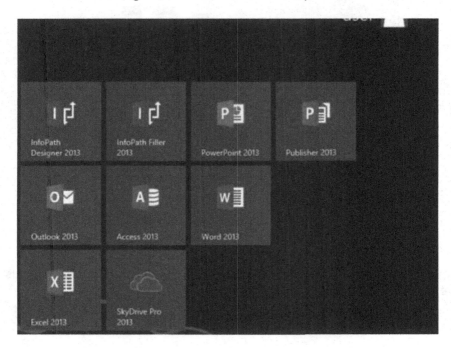

Once PowerPoint has loaded, select a template below to start a new presentation or select blank to start your own. I'm going to go with a mesh template below. Your most recently saved presentations are shown on the left hand orange pane below.

PowerPoint looks a little more complex than Keynote on the Mac. The tools are grouped into tabs called ribbons according to their function.

PowerPoint Tabs

In PowerPoint, the tools are arranged in tabs according to their use.

Home Tab

All tools to deal with text formatting, e.g. making text bold, changing fonts, and the most common tools

Insert Tab

All tools to do with inserting photos, graphics, sounds, movies, etc.

Design Tab

All tools to do with the look of your slide, e.g., the slide background.

Transitions Tab

All tools to add effects shown as slides change from one to the next.

Animations Tab

All tools to add slide transitions and add effects to text boxes.

Slideshow Tab

All tools to do with setting up your slideshow and running your presentation.

Adding a Slide

On the home tab, click "new slide".

Click where it says Click to add Title, add a title "Common Facts"

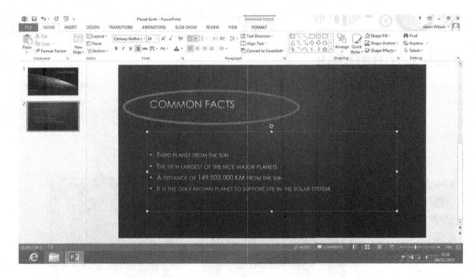

Add some text by clicking the "click to add text", use the text in the slide above.

Adding Special Effects
Slide Transitions

A slide transition is an animation or effect that is displayed when you move from one slide to the next.

To add transitions to PowerPoint slides you need to go to the Transitions tab.

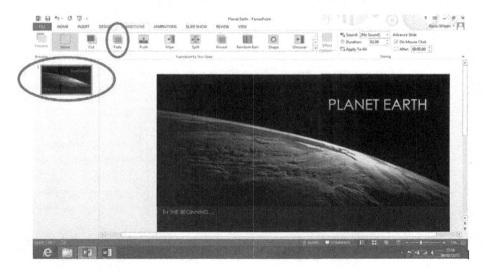

Click on the slide you want to add the transition to on the left hand column.

Click one of the transition effects. I'm going to use a nice fade.

Slide Animations

Looking at the slide below, let's say you wanted each bullet point to appear one at a time instead of all at once.

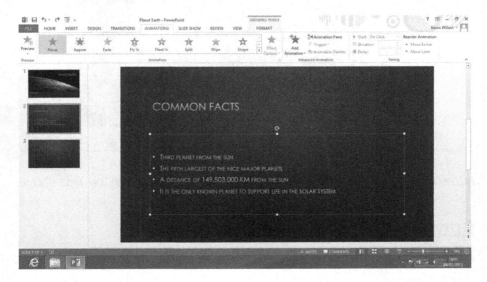

Click the text box you want to work on. In this example, I want all the bullet points to show up one by one. To do this, I am going to:

Select my Animations ribbon at the top of the screen.

Click on the text box containing the bullet points.

Click Appear in the Animations ribbon.

To view your presentation, press F5 on the keyboard.

Chapter 24

Computer Security

Anti-Virus Software

Anti-Virus software is required software for any computer. But in the case of Anti-virus software, more is generally not better. The reason is that more than one can often interfere with the other. A lot of this software is sold pre-installed on the machine you buy and is offered on a subscription basis. So you have to pay to update the software. It makes sense to have good protection, but there is a lot of good inexpensive or even free anti-virus software out there.

Windows 8.1 comes with its own version of anti-virus called Windows Defender. In addition, Microsoft Security Essentials is also free to download and use on a home computer. If you are running Windows 8, you don't need to install Security Essentials so you can skip this section.

To download Security Essentials, open your web browser and go to the Security Essentials website www.microsoft.com/en-gb/security/pc-security/mse.aspx.

There you can download and run the installation. Then follow the instructions on screen.

When you click download you will get a prompt similar to the one below; make sure you click run.

Follow the instructions on the screen.

Family Safety

In Microsoft's view, everyone who uses a computer should have a Microsoft account so that they can log on and have their own settings and own set of resources and restrictions. So why not start them early? To this end, they offer *child accounts*. A child *can* be signed up under a normal account or a child account. Everyone can customize their own experience with Windows. But Family Safety enables children to build their own environments with settings, apps and so on directed at their level. More importantly the parent administrator can direct what they can or cannot view, impose limits on their time online and get reports on their activity. The screen below shows how to add a child account

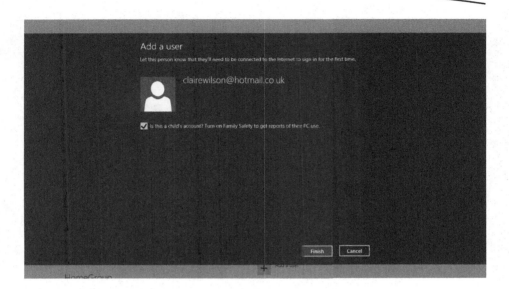

Each child has their own password protected access to devices that you share with the child. For a child account, an email address is not required. Each child's access can be custom fit for the individual. After you have created the account for your child, you will see the screen below and by selecting that person, you will be able to configure that user's account.

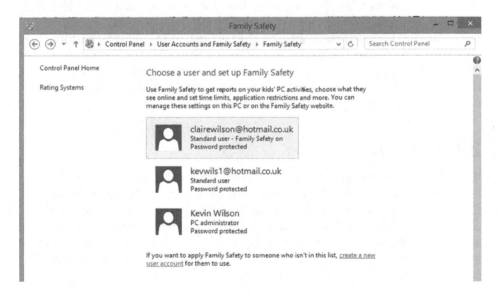

You can use this screen to add more user accounts as well. Note that one parent needs to be the administrator. After selecting the account, you can set up your child's access using the fields in the following screen.

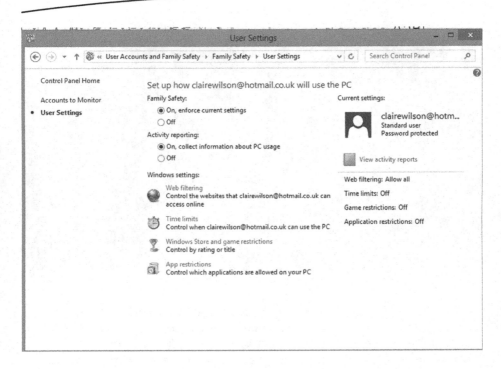

As you can see, you can choose to get reporting about the child's PC usage. You can enable web filtering to control the type of websites and content that the child can view. You can set time limits to log them out after a specific time. You can impose restrictions on their access to the Windows Store and restrictions on gaming and you can control what applications are allowed on the PC. Finally, you can enable Family Safety on the computer and monitor the activities of the child with a normal user account. A child account is not necessary to get activity reports on a user account.

Backing Up

If you have ever lost data because of a computer glitch or crash you know how frustrating it can be. So we all need a good backup strategy. While there are many options available today for backups in the corporate world or for people, who may have a lot at risk, price matters to most of us and so be wary of offers for X amount of free space in the cloud. I'm going to go through the strategy I have found that has worked well over the years and it remains a good inexpensive option today.

First of all, go buy yourself a good external hard disk. This is a small device that plugs into a USB port on your computer. Below is a typical specification for an external hard disk

Plug your external drive into a free USB port on your computer. Activate the Charms bar, and select Settings. Then click the Control Panel and select 'Save backup copies of your files with file history' under System and Security.

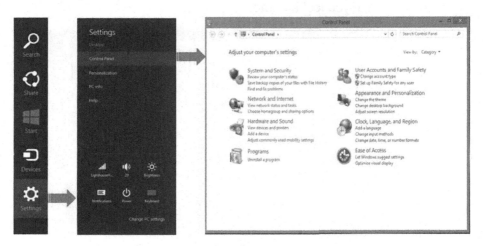

To activate File History click 'turn on'. Windows will automatically start saving your files to the external hard drive.

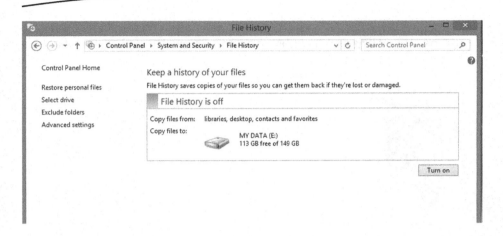

To restore files click 'restore personal files'.

Use the left and right arrows at the bottom to navigate to the date of the back up when you know your file(s) were still ok.

Then in the Library section double click in the folder the file was in. For example Pictures, if you lost a photo.

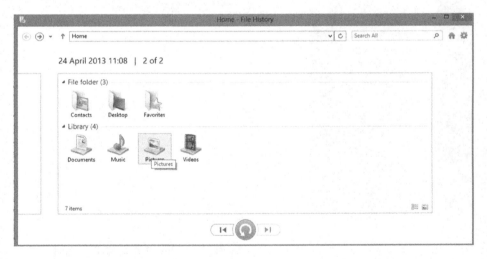

Select the photo and to restore it, click the green button at the bottom of the window.

Also as an extra line of defense, important files can be saved onto a flash drive or memory stick like any of the ones shown below.

These devices don't hold as much data as an external hard disk but can be useful to hold important documents or photos. They can hold 1GB – 256GB.

These devices are also great for moving files to another computer. For example, if you have a photograph or document you want to load up on a friend's computer.

Chapter 25

Computer Maintenance

This chapter deals with many of the issues of basic maintenance both from a software perspective and a physical perspective.

Windows Update

Your computer may be set to automatic updates already, but if not and you for whatever do not want automatic updates, you should at least get important ones. You can get updates to Windows for bug fixes and the like by searching for "update" in Settings and clicking on *Install optional updates*.

Disk Defragmentation

Data is saved in blocks on the surface of the disk called *clusters*. When a computer saves your file, it writes the data to the next empty cluster on the disk, even if the clusters are not adjacent. This allows faster performance, and usually, the disk is spinning fast enough that this has little effect on the time it takes to open the file.

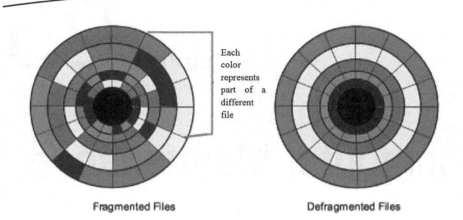

Each color represents part of a different file

Fragmented Files   Defragmented Files

However, as more and more files are created, saved, deleted or changed, the data becomes fragmented across the surface of a disk, and it takes longer to access. This can cause problems when launching software (because it will often load many different files as it launches) so bad fragmentation just makes every operation on the computer take longer but eventually fragmentation can cause applications to crash, hang, or even corrupt the data.

To defragment the disk in Windows 8, activate the search and type 'defragment'. Make sure you click Settings to tell Windows to search in the system apps as shown below.

Select the drive your system is installed on, this is usually C. Click Optimize.

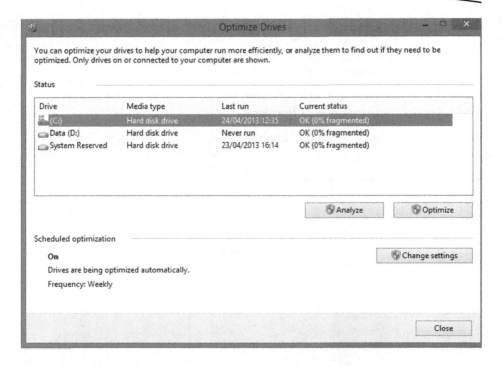

This will start defragmenting your disk. It will take a while.

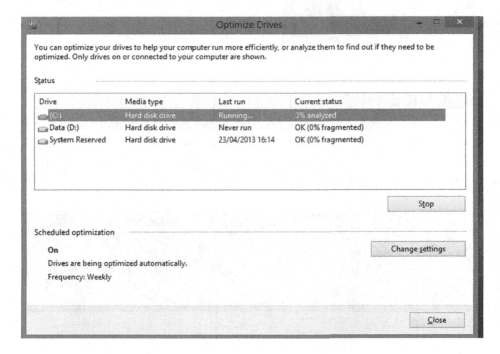

Manually Checking Your Hard Drive for Errors

In Windows 8, Microsoft changed the way we fix corruptions so as to minimize the downtime due to disk checks.

A new file system was introduced called ReFS, which does not require a manual disk check to repair corruptions.

From the desktop, click the File Explorer icon on the taskbar, right click local disk, click properties, select the Tools tab, click Check then click *Scan drive*.

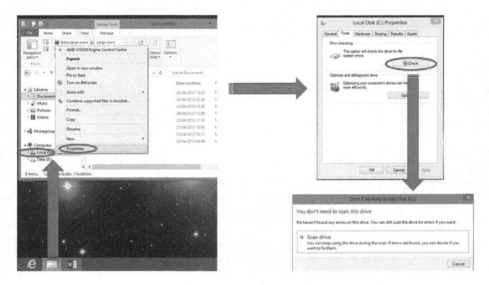

Disk Clean-Up

Over time, Windows gets clogged up with temporary files from browsing the internet, installing and un-installing software and general every day usage.

Open up the search and type 'cleanup', make sure you select 'Settings' to tell Windows to search in the system utilities.

Click 'free up disk space by deleting unnecessary files'

Select drive C, click ok. In the window that appears you can see a list of all the different files and caches. It is safe to select all these for clearing.

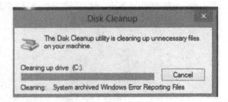

Once you are done, click ok and Windows will clear out all those old files.

Automatic Maintenance

Windows 8 introduces a new feature that allows you to schedule and run Automatic Maintenance on your computer such as security updating and scanning, Windows software updates, disk defragmentation, disk volume errors, system diagnostics, etc.

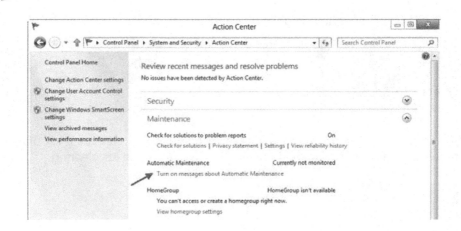

Start-Up Programs

Hit Ctrl-Alt-Delete on your keyboard and select Task Manager from the menu. Click more details if you don't have the screen below right.

Click on the Startup tab. Most of these programs can be disabled with the exception of your sound, video and network devices.

You will also see the *startup impact*. This shows how much the program slows the machine down. These are the programs that show up in your system tray on the bottom right hand side of your screen. As you can see below this system is quite clean – only essential icons appear in the tray.

Keep Your Computer Physically Clean

Cleaning Keyboards

To clean your keyboard, unplug it from the computer, use a paper towel dabbed with rubbing alcohol (or diluted washing up liquid) and run the paper towel over the keys to remove all the dirt.

To clear dirt from in between the keys, a can of compressed air is a good way to do this.

Cleaning Computer Mice

First unplug your mouse from the computer.

Older mice had a ball inside that tracks the movement, you can remove the ball by twisting the cover ring counter-clockwise.

Remove the ball and with your alcohol rub the ball to remove dirt and grease. Also clean the little rollers inside with your paper towel.

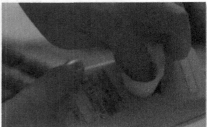

Put the cover back on and plug your mouse back in.

Newer mice are known as optical mice and do not have track balls. To clean these is much simpler. Unplug your mouse. Then, with your paper towel, use your alcohol to wipe the optical window, shown below.

Cleaning your Monitor

Modern LCD screens can be quite fragile on the surface so take care when cleaning the screen.

First, unplug your monitor and with a soft cloth dampened with some diluted washing up liquid start to gently wipe the surface making sure you remove dust and finger marks, etc.

Dealing with Spills

Spills and your keyboard generally do not mix. So, it is a very good idea to keep drinks away from the keyboard. If you don't follow this advice and have a spill, I have found that the best results come from shutting down the computer, disconnecting the keyboard and holding it upside down over a sink. If the liquid is sticky, it can pose real problems, so in that case, hold the keyboard on its side and run warm water on it. Then in either case you have to let the keyboard dry completely. It may not survive and you may be without a keyboard for a few days. And there is a reasonable chance of failure. Turning it on while it's still wet is likely to kill it. Even if it dries out, it may not make it.

Index

Get the eBook for only $10!

Now you can take the weightless companion with you anywhere, anytime. Your purchase of this book entitles you to 3 electronic versions for only $10.

This Apress title will prove so indispensible that you'll want to carry it with you everywhere, which is why we are offering the eBook in 3 formats for only $10 if you have already purchased the print book.

Convenient and fully searchable, the PDF version enables you to easily find and copy code—or perform examples by quickly toggling between instructions and   applications. The MOBI format is ideal for your Kindle, while the ePUB can be utilized on a variety of mobile devices.

Go to www.apress.com/promo/tendollars to purchase your companion eBook.